'AMPERSAND'

D P THORNTON

© Derek Peter Thornton 2025

Cover photo: Father & Son

The rights of Derek Peter Thornton to be identified as the author of this work have been asserted by him in accordance with the Copyright, Designs and Patents Act of 1988.

All rights reserved; no part of this publication may be reproduced, stored in a retrieval system, or transmitted in any form or by any means, electronic, mechanical, photocopying, recording or otherwise without the prior written consent of the publisher or a licence permitting copying in the UK issued by the Copyright Licensing Agency Ltd. www.cla.co.uk

ISBN 978-1-78792-115-3

Book design, layout and production management by Into Print
www.intoprint.net
+44 (0)1604 832149

Dedicated to:

Skylar Neese, Arthur Labinjo Hughes & Popcorn

*

CONTENTS

Ampersand **7**
World **8**
Injuries **9**
Epitaph to Arthur **10**
Dragonflies **12**
Be Happy **14**
We Had To Let Them Go **18**
What A Unique Bunch We Are **20**
Bring In The Dead **22**
Ashtray **25**
Vesica Piscis **28**
Physics of Ignorance **30**
It's For You To Know … **32**
Lili **34**
Moans, Groans **37**
Rushing To Be Rushin' **40**
Skylar Neese **44**
Broken English **47**
Colossal **50**

CONTENTS

Magpies **52**
The Hand **56**
Like **59**
4's 'n' Agnst **62**
Flyt **66**
Conscientious Objector **69**
Transmigration **72**
Virgo **74**
Black Peacock Butterfly **76**
And So It Came To This **80**
Et Tu **82**
Pristine **85**
Whywiz. 2024 **91**
Pooh Day **93**
Popcorn **95**
World Snooker Championship 2022 **97**
"The Legend That Was Dek"**101**
Tom Thumb **107**
Come (Song Of Avalon)**109**

AMPERSAND

Resembling a broken infinity
the ampersand reminds us that
nothing truly lasts forever
there is always an AND

&

An ampersand is a marvellous symbol
It says
"AND – I AM NOT FINISHED,
THERE IS MORE …"

My whole life is a great big
ampersand right now, & …

WORLD

Let us lift above yesterday –
Let us lift above tomorrow.

Turn your back on the sorrow
Turn your back on the hate – and then

Never turn your back on love
Never turn your back on love again.

To the world – archetype
Rise above and turn away!

Don't turn away from love
Don't turn away from love again.

A laurel leaf of love and poem
A sense of triumph – tears with joy
Never turn your back on love again.

Become the wishful thinking bard
Accepting the will of betrothal
Never turning your back on the empty soul
Never ashamed of the ocean of tears.

INJURIES

    Sciatica – back op
    dermatitis [dry and sore]
    knee spasm
    [movement limited to cane]
    moments of paralysis
              of left leg.
    Pain – lame – cane
    2 broken ankles

    *

    neck spasm
    head injury
    left leg artificial
    right leg – paralysis
    sciatica – bad
    walking
    working
    back op
    head op.
    Ankles broken –
    therapy –

EPITAPH TO ARTHUR

6 years old; Arthur Labinjo Hughes. Bless.
Died: 1am. 17th June 2021. RIP.
Killed by his relative parents; murdered and tortured.
In the West Midlands of England.
His words to the world the energy the spirit!
"No one loves me!"
"No one is going to feed me!"
How can this be? How could this happen?
The deeper feelings for the young boy
Knowing parents can abuse – who can you love?
To have the vulnerability of others – to be without
the immense dangers of time and place
so young without – so lost and wondered?
Where is the true help, the hope, the spirit?
It is good when all is well and strong and fine and …
To be killed at an age of older and bolder and
I will *"FUCKING KILL YOU"*
Is right. Is the way to survive – is wrong when
it is what you have to carry in the mindset of being!?
But a baby child; strong and knowing? Like Arthur.
Defenceless. Timid. Reliant and seeking true love
in and on a planet of death to killing to devour and slaughter
disarranged to suit the civilisations of the soul
there then is the combat to adapting and overcome
what!?

Then to poetic words of 'non compos mentis' – for sure
to the hatred and despise of us all
And to them; the 'folie a' deux.
Rest in peace Arthur and I hope you find your true love
Please don't worry
Someone cares
and there you will be gifted with the light of truth!
Bless you young boy. X

DRAGONFLIES

Loss of marshes, bogs 'n' swamps.
A global decline in Dragonflies!
The plight has highlighted the loss
in the wetlands –
due to urbanisation
'n' unsustainable agriculture.
The vulture
when the scavenger invades
paid to price
with holy sexual vice
this is nice to know
as so it goes
away … saying
this was the day of the dragonfly
the swampy foliage
and damp to stream
wherever there are dragonflies
there are dragons!
Wherever there is population boom
there is soon to be an extinct species
releases of tumour
indignation 'n' aggression
where we will live to the Japanese end!

Not wood but escorts to the new world
without the past
without the nature of most
covered by humankind
having left behind; but brought on through
to you, to be, to serve
and remember
as the pets of the future
are cute and kind
covered by the reason for human behinds
then it is all well with the creator
as the sterile bland world recycled
is placebo to so many fathoms
beyond the calling
beneath the roots of
towards the death on
as so; called to arms
besmeared in touch
fallout and begotten
the death will never last
will be past

… and sods will live forever!

BE HAPPY

"Be happy, don't be sad," they said.
They had found each other in the ethereal heaven
a fountain favoured fecundity
beckoning to the shores of love.
Whilst all around they came from days of yore
five fold and four score
aloud and alive
to the youth and the young
the old and the strong
they came to pay their respects
to the living souls of two.
As they shared in the solace
remembered the days
the spring arisen
and summer bathed
so many gone and so many left to wonder
at the path of grace
a pace to squander
with pathos days
yearning for the souls of forgotten times
too painful to recall
too few to say at all
they loved and loved to the full
with joy they wandered into the fold
with dignity and forthright hope

they entered the holy rightful place
of many an infinite face
to light up the darkness with love cherished
to allow for the blind to see
it is all it takes to reach eternal heaven
be forgiven
never regret
always take the lonely path to salvation
and never stray in the arrogance of ego's vain
lust for murder
in plaintiff
in mastication
shall the honoured and righteous
fathom the further
the afterlife of fibre
in the shining stars of immortals
secured in sequence of birth
to an almighty triumph; gleaned
seemed to be galactic
an answer to the unknown greatness
simple; there
earned and gifted
to be forever
not opposite
but, true

not enemy
but, through to the ultimate end.
There amongst the firmament
a vast collection of home
a given right to bid
by the solution to; no beginning; no end
but; is
will be
and gladly represented by
honourable truth
a proof intrinsic to the soul
heard and bathed
beyond solution
kind and warm
exemplary in all marriage
wed in space and time; eternal.
Heard and felt; external
needed and inspired
retired
to the holy grounds of light
together
they might chase the spangled astro
as they wish
complete and within the speck of cosmic atmosphere
Then they have journeyed to heaven
there they have found a once living love
between themselves

and there, they have reached a happy home
amongst the infinite multitude of many.
This is the story told –
To "Be happy, don't be sad," they said.
And those who disrespect themselves with others
burn in the fires of eternal hell and are gone; no more!
It is better to be born fighting and watching yourself
than to find others to damage
you can reach an afterlife it seems.
Streams of glittering omnipresent hooray!

WE HAD TO LET THEM GO

It felt like we had to let them go.
They seemed happy together.
The sense of the journey to find each other
Had been completed by a time
We seemed to have to let them go.
The sacred celebrations of a life well spent
To the failing hour
and the unknown path
to love; through love
holding and binding a gravity together
in signs of brighter hope –
glory, the days of life remembered
to find and see
the people of creation
an evolution to immortalise
a seeming smile
passing by
forgotten on many days
to be remembered
as the feeling of life-force
brings thankful truths
abound in use of
moments, few –

a still magic
to hope and understanding
the being of there
and a face to bear
the ultimate place in and beyond
gone, but still the essence of emotion
feels as they are
a light; so bright
to brighten up the dulling dirge
within brilliance majestic triumphant
it feels like we have to let them go
as they know respect is shown
they smile and share amongst us joy
a living strength; gives thanks and heals
when it is done
at a universal journey's end.

WHAT A UNIQUE BUNCH WE ARE!

Walking about with our egos 'n vanity
seeming to realise the possibility of one's-self
only needing the quiet feeling of being –
not seeming to know –
only; aware of the singular space
due to creation's dice.
And its limitation to fulfil the pleasant help
so the world remains in vain
as the sense of decent democracy
strangles the reason for being who we are
as it seeps through the value
now and again –
pours through the pores of virtue
to show us the nature of our state
in representation of poison sliding out of a wound
only to know we walk on bones
and look to the same moon
then freedom loosens the grip on pain
lets in the vain and the vanity
compared – to parallel hopes
when one does good, good is paid
it is the only thing one can do to help
it would need a turmoil of universal catastrophe
to let go the hold on moral – it needs to be set free

to walk the streets of hate that's crime and sin
to take its last breath and die
as the new generations live in the golden age of
genuine pulsating freedom
rid the chains – rid the bondage –
rid the veins of deterministical horror!
This our war – to die for and let the others thrive.
Been alive – so unique – so immersed in weakness
time brings the strength to know
to survive – what is this, a team? Woe

I'll read it to you afterwards –
after the day has gone
after the dying of the wrong
after this and after that
and after you your sickle prattle!
What a unique bunch we were.
Let it go to the maker
and heal the wounds of evil!

So smug & opulent
after new born
15 month
Arthur 6 years old; children; murdered.

BRING IN THE DEAD

Bring in the dead, the wonderful dead
Bring in the bread, the wonderful bread
Bring in your friends, all wonderful friends
Bring in the end, the wonderful end.

Bring in the truth, the marvellous truth
Bring in the proof, the rightful proof
finding aloof the sense of all known
coming apart in the dance of alone.

Never again seeing the sights of the night
never again putting what's wrong to be right
Bring in the hope, the fantastic scope
which leads to the journey made by most.

Bring in the love, the ominous love
Bring in the dove, flying out up above
Bring along so many times and its past
seeing the light of the future at last …

Never again would the memories fade
outside in the forest and the ever-glade
Take on the senses, recompenses and fire
Never deny the everlasting desire

To see and be, alight and alone
seeking the bubble burst in a moan
taking the time to develop the strength
running the step, achieving all lengths

To bring in the gladness, sadness and stealth
taking the cover to safety and health
Bring in the song the wonderful song
making life long and worth it.

Bring in the spirit, a wonderful spirit
Bring in those in it, the wonderful 'innit'
Bring out the compassion, lesson and learnt
Bring in the damaged, dishevelled and burnt.

Time takes its toll on the diamond rock 'n' roll
Time brings its age, regardless of faith
Time tells the time, as you pull on a finger
Time gives you movement, don't have to linger.

Bring in the tread, the truth trod and threaded
Bring in the web, which holds most together
Bring the utmost, feeling of dread
Take down the net and heal out the head.

Bring in the climate, the mountains of power
Bring in the bow and the feminine tower
Seek out the doing, the don't and the won't
Take out the necessary greed of the show.

Don't be afraid of the senses of will
of war and the death of the energy pill
Take out the time to trouble the soul
Never forget, the forgetting role.

Bring in the men, the marvellous men
Bring in all women, the wonderful women … etc

[This could go on forever. An infinite chant.]

ASHTRAY

COMbination
coming into the rumble roar of the inner city
plainly searched out for the pretty
hence, the façade has won
giving seance to the violet cock-fightings it would be
inside a latrine not a temple being
I find the less I do
the better it is for the planetary world
the more *others* go to bed and sleep
the better it is for her.
Did you know:
Thomas Hardy was born on my daughter's birthday?
2nd of June
and Rudyard Kipling died on mine; 18th of January – so
I go about my life
like Canned Heat at Woodstock
I play my guitar with Jimi Hendrix
as it sounds out of tune
so too, is
Greek in spirit
Pneuma'
Pneumonia
… breath …
the last vestige

the last refrain
into the toilet and ashtray again
tho' in loss of romance
and the pitched proceeding of love and sex
without less
without the best
romantic fascination
in the holy colours of
naphthalene blue
in hue
in wisdom
and a diverse liberty
They can be free
a little while
at least

Just find the difference
and never mind the cow
cud
crux
or foundations to the holy soul
just be it now
and then
then it becomes from what is birth
whatever be-cometh

it will
and why
one cannot see
is as
one is dead.
One becomes the great mighty holy dust
which covers the sun
and dots out the day
anyway
it is not your fault
you can be
as the one true
sense becomes a diversity
in synchronised relative destiny
without the bible book
without the hatred look
the death of nature
and the Artificial Intelligent
formulae
to never have seen an animal
in your life
till the collapse of innocence
an apocryphal of books
never does
and never looks.

VESICA PISCIS

In German: *Fischblase!*
as is the fish bladder
climbing up the ladder...
in sacred geometry
like many a crop circle?
She said, "It is not about the atmosphere of the energy
coming from the sky firmament,
it is about the effect of it magnetising from within the earth."
[like the iron filings on top whilst the magnet draws beneath
for the effect of movement and shape.]
Thus, the message of Gaia – the organic planet.
As the fruit of life is erection and boo
shaped like the womb of Mandorla
the Italian almond.
It all comes to the worthy effect
of worship
and principle
then towards
thus the given creation
to create
to anticipate
all futures
to be rife, ripe and full of humanity
can it be stilled to the stop
can it take the will

reaching the drop
loose, then, toss, then more
… and it is the stubborn outright signal
of the Goddess … betrothed
besmirched
belittled and misunderstood…
as mystery can't help it
as it does
it will do
as we are then we will change
and we become the Neo-race
of libertines
to go where no one has before…
fishing…

PHYSICS OF IGNORANCE

When a child is born…
the sense of the older path is natural organics
then they have their own sense of their own lives
for the future, knowing of parents' experience
hence, they don't need the lessons of you to enlighten them
they already know, then they have to understand their future!
As the beginning of cremation allows for Carolina
reaper death to die,
of the elder in knowledge of interplanetary
with the over-population in experience,
as a living cascade of duty
is the answer to the beauty, the foretelling and compelling
of ignorance and the solution of a disrespect of the species
which has dignified the laws, parented to younger hunger
and driven the truth, into a truth which allows galactic thunder
into an anarchy of chaos and blunder wonder
which is the excuse of an unknown universe
and the hopes to know the larger aqua family
and mass influence is thriving
in the sacrificial end-dreams of the sacrificial utopian
leaving the strand of umbilical,
cutting the severance of stranger aliens
to connect to a global relative natural in gene and DNA
giving rise to hope, the pope, the scope, the dope
and holy sanctuary minuscule insanity

without death, war, pestilence and famine
deterring the sacred knowledge of the journey of birth
on earth as it is in heaven
Then, what you have knowledge of, will be known
and what is to be, will be.
Know, then, it is the turn of the known to see the birth
of seeking to know
as they already do and will be known…
seeming strange, disarranged and secure in the instinct
of being better than you were … better than YOU are …
seemingly setting the beams of sanctuary alight!
as it's the anger of the selfish generations which
has been blasphemous of such physics of ignorance
physical attracting and dubious tyranny!

IT'S FOR YOU TO KNOW...

It's for you to know…
and for me not to have to say …?
*"I don't believe in sex,
women do."*
We are taking off ourselves
where no one is innocent
and no one is guilty
we have found liberty
as all that is left is *'it'* –
the question is as to *why?*
would be Y, Epsilon
in the age of Aquarius
which is a revolution in terms
of time and the elements of
water and air –
I am yew
you are me
I am an oak tree
you are free
I am the lotus leaf
the pond, beyond
the lake, the fake, intention
to be

in all
liberty and fraternised by
the world gone insane
as it remains on a planet
'et petere'
petulant, rude, behavioural.
A traveller is one who takes his life with him
Whereas a tourist leaves it behind at home for a while.
Don't be addicted…
don't be the scales
be the *SWORD*
as in the Kwami helix of Deoxyribo Nucleic Acids
watch ya P's n Q's
as loneliness is ugly
in this invasion.

LILI

Black moon Lil
she's a taboo; you too
in hidden true sexual desires
for the world to avoid
in ridicule and abandonment
as for those of privilege
the like of earned, created
gifted and fortuned
also, not realising the balance
of those that have and those that have not
then they seem to be selfish in the ignorance
of heroism; a dance of fame
letting out the sympathy again
as the opulence of money and security
in a world of religious righteousness
seeming to seek piety
then comfort for the few
as the talent of you
is wasted and affronted
by the loaded dice of time
and places, disgraces
in the humanoid race
to form the patterns
in triumph and trumpets
like it or lump it

Thus, there must be another way
there must be a better day
there is a better end
to the friendship of hours of honour
thus, the bus creeks down the road
of a fucked up load
as the world cannot be judged
unless, the mud sticks
and little by little
it mixes with the hexes
less…
music, money, fame and honey
to share with the sorrow of loss, death, murder and war
then, we can see the idea of the Alice band
to lend a hand; if you can
and kiss the world goodbye!
I like nonchalance
not to have to exert myself
nor insinuate; be explicit; exert oneself
then all places pricks up its ears
and listens for a while longer
going back to the personal styles
of egocentricity; ego-feeders paying for
electricity and unimaginative hope
we live with the answers and WILL

solve all problems of the apocryphallic
in the great lexicon
to belong, remain among
sing your song; lullaby …
Also walk the streets
sometimes in
worldly loneliness
as the world of annoyance
shows you your age
and self limitations
to vex the Dis and taxing
to wallow in your dung
done, then surely, I might
find what I have left behind.

MOANS, GROANS

...a writer
'to put things right'
so others are wrong?
solemn rushing was a wrong-headed
in all the senses of a fantastic procedure
saluting the pressure of worthy endeavour
making through the times of superior hope
then we are saviours in battle with the destiny
of a great dynamic
flowing forever lush
by the understanding of finality
to the death star
to never having to face death
to never die
but return
to Hermes strategists
to the infinitesimal of triumph, talk
with the holy strength of being addicted to life
never seeming to let go
never returning
to let you know
but, still, it talks beyond and incensed to;
this the nap of sleeping divas
as angels
lessen the vertex of all understanding

heights, achievements, salvation and love
then she is a goddess of Venus
shaped like the centaur Chiron
with a wound which never heals
with water and air; Makemake?
As to the yon I?
an isolated dark moon
as yonder swoon to black Lillith
'mongst Mars the king of war
in telling one's fortune precise
then let the lice crawl over the carcass depths
clear it!

*

Clean It!
macabre death of queen
life – idiot – nothing!
Is a spermatozoon seed alive?
Amongst the 100 million others?
Precious the gift of creation!
Universal astronomy;
"As sex workers;
too much of one thing.
Is not enough."
brought forth then
as the serpent carrier

O few curse
and the terms of true love; are
a total equality
for all
based on an equal understanding
of everything google
and everything known to modern man
Did you feel that?
Equal to the fucking prattle
who does not feel nor need
to feed on the given terms of being
still without the hope of thought and unique clarification
we don't have
deep seated loneliness incessantly drunk with the times
going going…gone by…
back to the creation
to conscientiously avoid
the void
void
fill, cleanse
fulfil the desires to know
to be
moans, groans, rants and ravings…!
stay safe, keep well, stay warm and sleep well….x

RUSHING TO BE RUSHIN'

The trees if you please
to the great grand apple
through-breed in thread
of time and life
be it dwarf or miniature
known for the wisdom and knowledge – green
in love and appreciation of fertility in abundance – red
Saturn apple; good health and happiness – less
simple summer days as the summer sets.
Forget about that one; death's an inconvenience.
As a conscientious objector,
rushing to be rushin'
like the non-freedom of all space junk
in a dislocated life style and outcome
in depth and colour as Australian soil
a beautiful terracotta red rusting
to be and the 200 thousands more
the changing children of the future
as the stasis is done and virtual
truth turns out to be
stranger than fiction
as slaughter becomes laughter
without the S
then guess…
it will be?

Likely naturalless with AI robots and aliens
it will be bound to human decision
it will be moved towards the challenge of progress
and can never return to the damage of the past
at last taken to the everything
which does not go
but is
in witness to all sacred truth
tho' whispered in the mind of the lost
it will cost
as 'they' free themselves from time
from death
from war
from a balance of ill will
it becomes the scales
measuring the principle of why
answered if you like by insight and knowledge
enlightenment and experience of many returning souls
of the soul returning
as it returns again
returning, until, it is free from the nightmare
of a condition of humanity
which does not fear
until the final rights
then it is simple

and enjoyment is the rule
a future paradise of the journey of love
which is the passage of mighty climates
to no end, to no betrayal –
no need to defend
the rights of man
the rights of her
the rights of humanity…
watch out for the space junk, again
my friend, a friend
is cured and cloned
doppelgänger and waffled
pleasant in extreme
as the world of bodies
knows itself
and will be like this; before it changes
and the fashion changes
as the senses
are the moving mutant
virtually trapped in a digital world
dancing with the algorithms
jiving!
The answer is us/them
there is no one else –
but you
must be me…in spirit

and in health
I delve into blasphemy and curtail the sanctions
till I can return a righteous soul
watching the fantastic of exciting times
with it taken in its stride
all holy pride and immense whore
done…love is the message;
without it, *'it'* is but sex.

SKYLAR NEESE

Murder in Texas in January at Walmart?
Seemingly the terms and methods of such …
but, this is ridiculous and horrific –
to trust some friends, to the end
and there fall foul to there evil ways
to the devil to Satan's shit!
Astonishing, a bit …
too disgusting all possibility
to see such disgrace
such murder lust
on the innocence of friendship
brings to bear the distrust of a fucking human
being, been, gone and lean
in all arrangement of one
the forgotten song of so many people
victims named by the perpetrator
who has no fill
be it a possession of will
by the nature of darkness
by the power to kill
being a monster in hideous disguise
the lies of a million times
the loss of kind
as the 'it' makes you feel okay
then 'it' has to feed!

As the world moves on and through
as others get clear and live
as the deal is done
and others have fun
for now … until it has to feed!
It might be you …
it could be yours …
ruined
ruined many
by the ominous beast which controls the fear
allows a lovely life for this
then takes to destroy the pitch
allowance like
as the truth is black damned
as the pain is circulated to human hearts
'it' starts to allow, need, let it live –
then. Gone.

*

*"You are the rock of my life
'n the light which shows me the way."*

*

I offer my condolences
and wish the world was clear

on knowing 'they will get theirs'
'n do –
and you will live beyond in the clear world
heard and knowing –
with love and loved ones
'it' should be shown a death row
then a humane injection to death
annihilated like the braver stars
as the heaven is light in the fibre
and those who kill this manifestation
go to oblivion
where it hurts
to never exist again
anywhere – any place
no sign of being representative of the human race
gone!
To the everlasting pain!
Non!
Never again … beyond infinity!

BROKEN ENGLISH

Anon ... and on ...
to an unchained melody
fellowship or remedy
or just bust, lust to the tusk
and task of basking in the dark
of the light, tonight;
thus, just in sight
shite ... possible to indite
a right to see the pleased and be
broken, spoken with delight
alight the gymnastic bile
through-breed – dun
a bun for lunch
crunch!
There goes the charabanc!
Lang de slang for singing
the hurtful truth and bringing
abuse to pain
again ... anon ...
cremation and noise of business
2000 degrees Fahrenheit for 3 hours
dust ash and crust
to find DNA in the rust?
Read it your Miranda rights
as the choke is around hybrid bone tight

the only legend is time
and time has its own understanding of 'things'
to be the things to see
the things that are and the things that shall be
Bowie
in a peloton of the main group of riders
to epiphany in mourning glory
hence the only winner is time's to will
the bill of forgiveness
justice and jurisdiction
then the senses have the hallow hope of redemption
and compensation
hence, anon, gone and wish to hell the others are paying
Ex morte vita
out of my death; new life.

*

North Thornborough henge is up for sale!
200,000 knicker!
Quicker still
to sale and bail out the flora and fauna
left to homage and rummage in the path of righteousness
less

we wallow and trespass
on those that trespass against themselves
camp wood
could, should and be free to the universal sight
of ancient times and modern rhythms
to rap and slap and spell it out to joyous crowns
in all village towns
pleased to be of service
as the nation resurfaces and finds
the broken china
Russian dolls and African sin
bin! In the bin and done …
… anon.

*

all fun of the fair
wrestle your way through life.

COLOSSAL

Society ignores itself!
But it is aware it is there.
To consume
to consumption
and consummation
we are here to signify
our insignificance
if you can
dance
celebrate
before it is too late
and the world changes
as we falter and alter the outcome
and outrun the times and the terms of a temperament which
never liked you
never heard you
never tried to tidy the truth
and seek the miss
find the kiss
and enjoin to a glorified resemblance of knowers
that it was;
a Ziziphus spina christi
which bleed the Messiah's head

as a holy thorn
torn and worn
by the conceit of prophets
the elite of finance
a momentous cascade of fear
to be afraid of the truth of covenant
one must have a bad mind
if one kills!?
as an event horizon
straight into a black hole!
To suck up the remnants of times
gone past at last to the peace of darkness;
which is not kind but evil here;
It been manicured, gentrified, commercialised and sanitised
to the comforting end ...
as the starlight gaze is appeased
and the show of chemical colour and astonishment is
adjusted to the journey of COLOSSAL silence
and beautiful infinite nothingness.

MAGPIES

Okay so there I was feeling strange ...
so there, I went for a small walk down the street ...
from there I returned
and peered out of my door ...
there on the roof tops of houses
was a load of magpies.
Arrayed in black and whites
with the hue of shiny silver blue.
I counted; the song;
1 for sorrow
2 for joy
3 for a girl
and 4 for a boy ...
5 for silver, I counted ...
6 for gold ...
7 for a secret never to be told? ... Magpie ... !

*

What was that secret?
To me and to my mythology
it was the secret of death.
To die.
What was in store?
What could it mean?
Where do we go?

All questions of mystery and charm
All feared and weird and warn!
All to be worked out and on ...
when one is not here!
... and gone ... !?

*

I had know someone who, one day had
7 magpies outside his home;
he had been ill for a while,
and he up and died.

*

I felt funny, unwell, strange ...
then, I saw an 8th bird!
To my sense of surprise
There was more than death!
Some of them came together
and squabbled!
Some they flew away and to no avail
did they budge from there representation.
I then felt the change to my system
I urinated, many times, phantom pissing
like my whole system was crashing!
Then the headache, I could not cough
it hurt ... it ached ...

I went to bed, to rest.
I broke into sweat and fever.
Cold.
I slept, awoke in angry pain
I tried to supply myself; to drink water
Then my heart doubled me over
and I sensed the depth of pain
in my chest …
I said, "It is my heart?"
to which it threw a great void
a lapse, a chasm of nothing, nowhere … pain …
twice.
I knew to fall on the floor would be not enough
then, it ceased, thankfully …
I lay back to rest and sleep … ?

*

I was very fragile the next day
as I was told, "You have been warned!"
a stroke, a heart attack? Perhaps
if you are not careful
I thought of fish and fruit … !
to cut down on consuming junk;
… of the 8 magpies, how they fought to move one
to make it 7.
nearly, a totem sign …
of omen proportions?

I felt myself ache
my head … ?

**

THE HAND

Ranting 'n' raving!
Moaning 'n' groaning … !
… this is my poetry x
today 'n' yesterday … forlorn x
then it is to being apoplectic –
towards the way others can look at me?!
I try to understand, then my inner self
sees the way it would about oneself:
How one knows inside; what others do not,
about me.
Not them x
The hand is shown
and says speak to it!
It says a rage of temper red
flowing through my veins
into the rains of sorrow
in drowning out of sadness
with alcohol mistress mine
there the happiness is false
but it is funny enough to be true x
Furious!
At the human race of conformity and comfort!
Hurt and troubled by the stereotype of mediocrity
seeming to delve deep into the broken dreams

and have the sense to reason with a rational hope
for futures present; laughter in condition
seeking incandescence
applauded by the greater masses and
higher beings given the chance to dance
to a freedom trance of luck in love x
an anger of aerate
a confusion of the state of terms
to which is a pleasant knowledge to exist
and rant!

*

My moaners!
My words
my life
inside 'n' outside; amongst
one has to know the way
about the simple outcome
which appears when one has waited
"it comes to those that do."
so the hatred sea of turmoil 'n' pressure
seeks the lesser
as the parting of the waves
saves the anger of a thousand destinys

And troops the colours of hope 'n' faith, then
love – the lifetime love
to rise above
to understand
to cherish in making of
then listen; and the voice of the one speaks;
deep and far beyond
into moments of loudness; madness!
Damaging the world's earth planet
with bad apples 'n' starvation –
until the poetry rates the raving
and it is true –
it belongs to you
as the the furious hand clenches
as it strokes the pain away
soothes the hungover
and never leaves the limp of expression
to use – to write – to capture; a sight
for sore eyes
lessen the limits, and open to the elements
of all helping hands –
we must live as another
then we are
then everything will become.
Impossible … to do?
Being me, being you x
livid.

LIKE

To like, not to have to love
with love, the opposite could happen
Hate.
So let's finally share with the strength of opposites
and seek the trouble of like –
to like: then this is to dislike.
I like this but I don't like that!
Hence it is almost on the fence
of defence when the turmoil of emotions
come to the fore
and there, the door of perception –
election and perpetration of all things liked
might find the divine nature of love is
to be in the straits of diminish
thence to ask for help
to ask for the nature to support
is the downward spiral of prayer
as it is not fair to ask for to be liked
it's enough to share in the sense of faith
religion and gods
and even understand why love is a good understanding
for reason, rationality and restorability
can't make it up as you go along …
in the sense of aphasia

in an amnesia of all this gone, wrong, longed for and smitten
then it is what the journey would state without such
one would be oblivious and ignorant of the lives lived
to an experience of status and respect
with control over themselves
when the world
has spat you out and the faith of being is the path
of simple taints
to scent, meant in fragrance
the telling of a floating mind
noises will claim the world!
"throw the myths into the seas
of the 'miffed'
through the mists of the missed."

*

hoping to privy
a life out of balance
a negative sorcerer who lives off
the expense of others!
Life in transition
asinine, then derelict
then seeming to understand the life at war
civilised violence
a life of killing each other
Nagasaki
Polarisation
Cybersquatting

then I have to full-fill the need to understanding
a land plain
gaining of salvation's truth
seen in the worth and birth
of all faction
thus letting-in the tractions
of all ages nearer
then clearer with time
unless born into times
changed;
times allowing the purer understanding
whilst the knowledge was fought for
the door; closes … closing … closed.
as the tears of decades in fears
subsides
and in its place; traversable travesty and believed
then one can be proud of the crowd cloud
enigmatic rainbow pirates
and shagging with no bloody lurex!
Fix and feuds
delicious muse
like and dis-like porn; a toothless dental fricative.
'Th'… or n x

"The universe demands balance.
For every Yin, there must be a Yang.
For every good, there must be a bad.
For every life, there must be death."

4'S 'N' AGNST

There's cool ones and there's shit ones
4's 'n' agnst
There's good days and bad days
4's 'n' agnst
when the time comes and it is good
it makes up for all the lost time
'n' the days when it is not so good; bad.
The virus brings but 4 'n' agnst
with some out of the way
'n' some needing to pay
but it can also bring illness n death
I would not wish such on anyone
apart from evil bastards killing others!
I would not like to see the world die of disease;
never the less; it can deserve its judgement
'n' dilemma;
towards a selfish state of monetary greed
'n' filth
towards a better world of better folk
of others who save lives and help in the hope
of peace on earth
with love 'n' glory
and everlasting stories of justice 'n' faith
lighting up the human golden gate
to supply 'n' help and deliver

the ultimate store of ideal beginnings
in moving into the future of respect and consideration
for humanity in the form of unconditional terms
of understanding the Zeitgeist of interplanetary proportions
'n' space aeronautics
of astronauts 'n' aero-smiths
in a solar system of knowledge; education 'n' heroism
then we can represent the 4 'n' agnst
instead of sex 'n' money; honey
of lusty love gone haywire!
Retire to the fields of gold
to the honourable and bold
never seeming old and young to the aspect
of variability beyond the truth of stars
'n' surface with a love for life in informative balance
like the offering of her holy sacred self
as the two headed beast turns into a garden of open
an no one needs feeding
'n' it is right to see the sight of Krishna blue.

*

with you and your noise
4's 'n' agnst
with you and your ploys
4's 'n' agnst

with hatred and wars!
4's 'n' agnst
with hurt 'n' pain; again
lame and limping
into blip and blitz
shit and shin
on the chin
'n' she was beautiful cause he says so
in his worship
of natural need
but to follow the greed
to seed the unknown
undone and followed
4 'n' agnst
the shallow
the depth of pretension
hawthorn
heathen
breathers
bastard and bugger
no more poisonous sugar
4's 'n' agnst
in most things
with most ways
it is not for you 'n' me
it has its place to find and be

but it would and cannot serve
this all 'n' everything
unless we find the answer to a mystery
which is not known
due to it been mysterious
but let it be told and set us free to roam
the streets of all cosmic homes
in dignity
in friendship 'n' knowing
we all know where we are going
to the 4's 'n' agnst
until, it peters out 'n' hears the mighty shout
which echoes through the strings of time
goes curious into the night
leads the way to complete 'n' utter right
to be to serve and live for life 'n' death.

FLYT *[the other day, the other night]*

To sit in the day, still …
looking out at the nature left …
the end of a blistering summer
when the autumn is slow and becoming grand
then it is to a visit from the ladybirds
in their signature of spots
on their backs
to tell the difference
with wings to take flyt
to safety
and might enjoy the daylight air
with the colour blue and green dark forest green hue
Flies!
the harbinger of death, salvation of scavenger recycled
the small and large bulbous; fly
as the Bee seeks the pollen from the flowered trees
the Wasps sting all opposition and die
from tearing their abdomen!
Watching the seagulls dash about from the sights of sea
with a sound so distinct
no words of human life could, should, may emulate
but, with the Pigeon
O sounding like the cooing and wooing of romance
and the petting dance of union

as their shit drops on ya window pane
now … the Magpies, one waits to see!
Such fantastic colours and silhouette
and yet one waits for 2 not 3
not sorrow or tomorrow or yesterday
on his tod, wait! here she arrives
with joy and the human sod is almighty lucky, by chance
giving thanks to the dark side of nature enhanced to see
Butterflies be, cherished
fluttering by
butterfly; the red admiral
and a crème de la crème in all her glory
to the aeroplane's story
running out of fuel
coming down in a contrail of despair
there! All birds in the feather of flyt
as the helicopter chapters to the sound
of a humming world, buzzing Bs
blessed in a damage of the ground
duck! In all his hurry, fuck! Look!
Swans in the flurry as the wing of the buried
and life, love, hope and the wonderful glory!
Of a marvellous story; told
set in modern times; be bold

set to amuse the rhymes and the times spent
of a sober poet drunk to be below it, all
at last at home in entomology and animal reason
as the start of the season, seasons and session
is the dying of a discontented winter
as this son of York!
What a full day was this sight of flyt.

CONSCIENTIOUS OBJECTOR

I am the conscientious objector; now ...
having been in life
an been a subjective –
as part of the experience
whereby, one is subject to the way
as the seeming sense of triumph
came about through immersion and commitment
to a cause of effect
which dictated the senses to understand
'n' recompense
the circumstances of being
allowed and willing
to share
'n' deploy
the motion of union
and meaning ways to spend
all time given
to cherish the terms
to delve, to want, to need
to feed, to bleed and fancy
the greed of many things
which could only
pass the time
in change and a passion

in manifesting the social
society
which makes the masses
takes the passes
relinquishes the dashes
lasses
and perfume of toil'et
then, yet
all brings back the tears of form
to sleep
and never have to wake
to the predicament
in sickness and in health

*

until, the pain
brings a gaping light of awakening –
thence,
one is conscientiously challenged
to educate the knowledge
incessant in the darkness fathoms
demented in the challenge of mind
seeing the truth
the proof of one's self
then, all becomes objective –
objects

but, saving the grace
of trespassing
saved now
by the moral of one's soul
a forever observing sight
not been subject
to the royalistics of concern
as individual universe
as a simple freedom
of viewing
a world subject to chapters
mapping out the masses
journey to salvation
knowing 'it' has been done
as one can slumber
in somnambulism of a developed ego
for a concerning conscientious future
of subject matter
and objective spirit.

TRANSMIGRATION

Life is not worth it
if everyone is not happy, especially the kids
I find it unfair, sad
until then how can we enjoy this
when there are those that don't, can't and have it taken away from them!
As the Christians say; because of a past life!
Why don't they fix it during transmigration then
so it doesn't have to be fixed here
where the lessons are harsh, murderous, repeated
God gives and God takes away; philosophy?
we learn nothing here, but to adapt and survive
we should be healed in the heavens before we are set to birth again
Then it is God
Incontinence, Incompetence, Intercontinental
… and there shall
be a roadway, a highway, and the
way of holiness, *(Wa-derek)*
it shall be called
the unclean will not travel on it,
but it will be the one who walks that way *(Derek)*,
and fools will not wander on it…

Isaiah 35: 8-10

Daleth Resh Kaf
D R K

Psalms 25: 4-5

the way (Derek)

as the proboscis and mandible is recognised
to suggest you know me
during your perception!?
Just a vocabulary of stereotypical analysis
and the Vulpine and Vixen are abused and hunted
by a hated human *been*!

VIRGO

Virgo in my dreams
it seems
to be weird
she was weird
but true ...
I, looked about in a French farm
and saw the sights of the countryside
I needed to see
there was a farmer
good to me
there was a strange farm
as alarm!
She came on the scene
there she was
just fine, it all felt she was mine
just right; there she was
a Virgo; strange middle-aged girl
who was the daughter of the farmer
then together
she moved towards his bedevilment, they came together
and taking, feeling, being, they
felt right
as the excitement of sex and lust
was exciting and just
she began to stroke her hair

and as the hair became less
she looked to me and showed me age
old age in her grey hair and looks change
then I squirmed and cute
she looked the same
shoot!
She was with me
I left the dream nonchalant
she watched as she seemed to wonder as to me exit
shrugging shoulders and seeming far and starlet
she waited for me to return

*

I did
she was with someone and putting food all over his body
like a food massage
I looked to her and she just kept the reason
He seemed to change and told me of her season
as that was the way she was
I asked about *us*?
She said "come to me when I need you"
I agreed and left the Virgo; strange wonderful farmer's girl
to her rituals
and countryside … it was all barnlike and organised
for welcoming
the dreamer.

BLACK PEACOCK BUTTERFLY

Okay ... in the dark
thus a butterfly flew about!
Dark of night?
No light?
Landed ... flying down the hallway
sat on my father's Royal Marine Korean badged jacket.
I went to have a look.
There was a large black butterfly!
Amazing ... never seen one before!
Thus it sent a shiver down my self
as I had been watching paranormal stories on t'box.
It sat there ... thus, I looked deeper
It had markings
but, they were black
the butterfly was all black!
An omen?
A sign?
Looked it up
an' fine ...
it could be the metamorphosis of a witch
come to pay me a visit
it could be a sign that someone may die
if it was my dad then he was already dead
perhaps he was visiting me from inside my head?
Just to let me know ... *what*?

That the spookys and watchers
were about in my space
they had come to trouble and disturb
they had come to tell me of my wealth
and my bad health?
The black peacock butterfly was still
resting – resting for the night
found a warm and welcome place
only I couldn't face the omniscient senses
when the black soul visits
and all is not well with the world
it is there to warn, to scorn and to destroy us

*

So, I got a glass and paper towel
captured it and took it outside
for a slight moment it sat on the verge of the glass
got its bearings
looking about
then flew to a wall
not at all
happy
perhaps disturbed
by the ominous figure of a human giant
I hope the black peacock butterfly found a place

to sleep
to keep
away from the folk-law
of such things
as death
black dark death
a harbinger of a future demise
so sad
the cast of a fellowship of termination
so bad, this truth of complete and utter fear
all clear
as the witch can find another person to visit
as death can wait for a planet's natural events
so beautiful but tumulus
just a warm place to rest
on me dad's old vest
at best
thanks, but no thanks
one sometimes has had enough of spectral hauntings
flaunting the spirit of peace 'n' condolence.
There should be no wrongdoing
on this planet by now –
the soul is seemly a sacred horror
if you get close.

*

I wrote the poem *Black Peacock Butterfly* on the 8th September, 2022, just a few hours before Her Majesty Queen Elizabeth II died.

"It could be a sign that someone may die."

The Black Peacock Butterfly had visited me a few days before.

*

AND SO IT CAME TO THIS
(what did I expect?)

… and so it came to this … in 2021
as the virus of the world takes president
as the spirit of the just leave without a trace
and the rivers flowing south a ponce the drift
cleft n cliff as the miff is solid
bowled and troublesome
taken and pranced through
below the terrible turmoil of fools
this is the downfall of many a year gone past
at last the negative fight for survival is right
on track
in pace and doubled
sought to borrow from the sacred dance
left to sorrow and the foreign grace
of problem relic
the gigs
the smouldering of polluted heavens
then with and without the Armageddon
the beast, the four, the whore and dragon!
Be it true and faithful set
let free the Satan soul
And yet; will be to symbolise
love – as it triumphs over prophecy
and profit

as the conglomerate of industrial firm
brings down the essence retold to fail
as it simply dies the pathos apoplectic
surmounts in calculation
n the nurturing strives to build again
as friends
as learnt
a burnt out cocoon of butterfly souls
for humankind; not Mankind?
It is how it feels and less that is done
it will find a place in the setting sun
no fun but serious – a nature to hold the mania's path
so it comes to this; as I ache with soulful pain
yearn in vain for the respiration of harmonious peace
at least the ideal world can exist in theory
the practice is real as the hoards of herds steal
the mighty covenant of heart
it "gets worse, to get better"
philosophys of unknown ghosts
shadow the wings of angels
as the few are left to forget.

ET TU

'Bereshit'; in the beginning –
and so the natives become a demonym?
The thematic toxic toxin tribe
as is the name;
I AM THAT I AM.
Tetragrammation
Adonai
El elohim
Shaddaul
Tzevaot
"as all is immune to your consultation"

*

Bowie.
'Telelestai'
'It is finished'
Aramaic …
to know what it may've sounded like?
Seemly to know
my death date: Nov 5th, 2046!
If I get that right let me know!
Always Thunder road;
Springsteen
always listening in to the silence

always a heartening noise; it's a noisy bastard their beast!
"Do you want to listen to activity?"
"I would rather listen to harmony."
The porpoise and the smell of a thyme swimming sea
blessed be pact scythe and all who sail in it
just one little bit left
et tu; 'you are one!'
you are too
you two
and follow the blue line to the prince of love
the quest is at best
to fathom one's heart
then it is in the centre of the breast
then it will forever be last
and last
aghast with horror
at the joy of sorrow
and the beating heart farthers to homage

*

brilliant the coming stars
oh so right the nearby night
in so much fear
as fright is the anxiety of souls

personally
something reaches its *n*eternal goal
preternatural; peter-out
with all the trimmings
to surprise the beginning; without end
easy to comprehend
and solve
just look to the signs and symbols and ponder
the solution
proof of salvation and worth
given one sleeps
doing the world a favour
and let the planet rest
& tu.

PRISTINE

Was the word ...
pristine

Pristine the day.
A mild beginning amongst the many.
Then, thus the timing ...
Here comes my brother; along the road,
crossing over; opposite is a sex woman
I fear for the unseen situation
and point her out to my younger brother
he sees her I fear; then she sees me, then him
then all is lost to interpretation; thus
she is lost and concerned for her feelings;
then she likes what she sees
as she crosses the way
looking at him
I lose the true timing of an inner passion
he is with partner; three children.
I have to challenge and battle in the competition
of desire and lust – bust! There is the end
'n' beginning of this day; thus we are good
brothers we know   x

*

On to the day and into the way
and many populate the earth now
many see and look and what is paid
for 'n' owned; is everything
in the sight of the soul
and the dreams are real
becoming bad ones; lacking in imagination
of a nation which is pristine to the eye
is like the cleaning of a home
everyday in every way …
and everyday
the soul dies
without love and understanding
without dreams of an utopian idealist social
world in league with time
and time is precious
as the way of time is settled
to sunny climbs and pristine functions
to too many people
and too many horrible buildings
with the on top bullshit
to inner slander and crime
wishing the world was a better place
and had turned out seemingly better
whilst they all know
as they are one

and the one is alone
as is the common sense of humility
and frozen depths
with eyes of distant pins
recognised out of the 'norm'
and into the storm of belonging
so your soul is not alone
amongst others
as she is now important
as the terms are different due to new
generations with intention to live
and survive
overcome and survive
with the pristine nature
of empty beauty
as the make-up covers the flesh
so the flesh is intelligent and insightful
to the oncoming strangers
with multi-pleasant prices
and stale concerns for others
in the endeavour of a common love
a know structure of routine
to the panoramic pristine
which holds a peace
pleasant and dormant
to the soul of the wild

then passion 'n' desire are inner chaos
it troubles the appetite
'n' worries the brain
as to the trouble of being
when in all knowledge
you must see the parliament of murder
the designated respect and trim
true to the few
and lost to the mind of horror
"I will see you again, tomorrow!"

*

I may never return to the sea
to be … burnt
to be loved
to need; like the need of all
I will need not to queue
for the price of life
to wander and squander
the health of life
as memories are crowded out
be yours
never been told
about castles and hotels
suicide bridges and the smells … !
gone; lost to the creator
the maker of this
a magic sense of bliss; pristine

with knowing; knowledge
a perspective delving divergence
into who? where? why? what?
This is your lot
as the beautiful blind girl knows her place
sending out the element to a human face
seeing without eyes
with black dog and cane
feeling truth; not the lies
for a fair usurped world
teeming with trot
the lot and moving on and far away
never to see another day
be fair, be right, be here!
Tonight and save my life
as it all seems out of my world
as it seems to be of their making;
hence; it is the way of the rich
stately; home; warm; bright
climate changing nights
and rock stars booze
they win, you lose
time to take up the space of given
a-liven and riven to the hilt of sorrow's sword

*

not against, not done, not knowing or
showing the defiance of rebels' youth

but proof to hope
then scope the senses of forgiveness
for they know not what they do
and neither do you.

WHYWIZ. 2 0 2 4

So it would be to the White Wizards.
Having seen them on Cley hill Wiltshire;
many years before in the 1992s
never having the right rudiments to shed its light!
Into the darkest night, when all was wrong –
they are the spectrum!
A Prism of delight when they are the White power
RE for red
When I was a boy,
OR for orange
I did boyish things…
GRE for green
Now that I am a man;
YEL for yellow
Do not say "he has gone"
VI or violet
but, that you are grateful
IN for indigo
he was here.
BLU for blue
assigned to the magic rainbow
the days of the week
to all senses and love meek
strange the seeming use of words?

as Slaughter, without the S
is laughter!?
So they are the wise ability
a cataclysm of stability
to find the subsidiary of terms
which can be the lesson
one can learn;
How it is then that they are Why
in all the brilliance of white wizardry
settled comfort, relaxed and safe
no need for the use
of the mind … too late
one has achieved one's fate
as the option to delegate
is complete
with the skill of delight
they are becoming
the right

*

Then I must learn to serve with strength
until we meet again
after so many years away
in a foundation of goodwill
allowing me to remain; forever a man.

POOH DAY *[Jan 18th]*

Me, I was born on Pooh day.
Like on the stack with Bukowski, Plath, Neruda & Dylan
(Thomas or Bob)
As I reside in the British library archives: Wetherby, Yorkshire
with *Meeting Famous People.*
someone must've read it?
A quill of bill, a thrill to still the soul of feather
like the pen of a female swan; never incorrect or wrong
"Then it seems like I'm getting older –
it's like I've seen it all."
I quote; Cheesy of Alvin & the Chipmunks.
Who were No.1 in the charts in Canada the day I was born.
'The Day The Rains Came' by Jane Morgan; here
and *'Smoke Gets In Your Eyes'* by the Platters in America.
And so the onus is on me, or you
It rhymes with the sense & feeling of pooh
as my nodes are my fears, in darkness and cleared
homophobia
claustrophobia
arachnophobia
isomorphically part of fortune
transmutational – transformational
'pars fortuna' is tangible as is a tangerine dream
magnum rectum opus anus
anus sphincter rectum; –

been alive 350 million seconds an' counting …
"perhaps it was a jinx – from a sphinx or a lynx?
that'll be it"; that'll be the day
derelict or this is the *'Way'*
a Bildungsroman when I come of age.
"to stand, when told to sit down,
to make a speech when asked to be quiet."
I quote; Johnny D justice.
To authorise the approval and support of authority
authoritarianism; say so, endorse
a green light sanction
signature.

'Winnie the Pooh' day 'cause AA Milne was born
on January 18th.

POPCORN

WHY DID SIX
6
NOT LIKE SEVEN?
7

BECAUSE

SEVEN ATE NINE
7   8   9

*

This is about watching Ronnie O'Sullivan win the Snooker World championship with such a charismatic ability; beyond words; beyond the normal common rascal that touches on the soul of God.
Amazing. Unbelievable; words fail me x

*

WORLD SNOOKER CHAMPIONSHIP 2022

So, Ronnie won it!
Equalling 7 times with Steven Hendry.
But what I saw and felt from the pelt
on baize; amazed at the way it was done,
won and the absolute genius of Ronnie O' Sullivan.
I have never seen the snooker balls
under such command!
"Come here!" and they did.
The total command of every shot
taking the red; blacks; taking the lot!
the flavour and panache of such a cue
if you have ever played; if you;
know what it is like – to control the white
a cue ball in name into the light
They all bowed to his master stroke
the balls, the crowd and the snooker folk
words such as "majestic" out of the commentary Virgo
words such as "sublime" from the Smurf magician
to know and to climb
with such ease and indifference to the struggle
seeking the solution to the soldier's bubble
once then to the strife of the table knife
worked at it like it was a day at the job
worked at it till the hair grew like a yob

and on to the brilliance to talk in riddles
out to the baulk end
and into the middle
pockets yearned and yawned
the exceptions of so
surreal a story
a fantastic voyage
there could be no better touch
so velveteen; so much …
blink and you'd miss it
as the others went out to piss it
remember how and where and why
you could never look deep into the tiger's eye
for granted and forlorn t'others
all of many a day
with sister and brothers
to see the ultimatum of a life's work
and study
come into play; thinking ahead; no worry
Thence it would be complete and done
underneath the table and on with the run
of many a figure broken and sworn
cues worn out and white shirts torn
to this then and that?
How is it done?
Don't ask the question

ask it for fun …
Practice. It's practice and natural talent
the combination of a thousand hours to see
a pleasant smile and pleasantry
only then doth the character and figure known
be; Ronnie the Rocket
by every pocket
be they not free, till the end
a cue tip to solve; a cue tip to mend.
And yet still with gracious wit and guile
bringing out into the world; in magnificent humours
a glorious smile
of magnitude and formidable skill
is this to be known, until …
a perfect arrangement of man and sport
never a shot taken in contort
and lo and behold;
yes to unfold
a righteousness witnessed
a god-given right
staying up into the middle of the night
all forgone conclusions and triumphant will
all of the green world
bows to his skill.

"Do you think you can upset the order of the universe and not pay the price?"

[Gump from Legend]

"THE LEGEND THAT WAS DEK"
[A quote from the actor Steven Hartley to our kid]

He said "the legend that was Dek"
When I was at school
a long time ago …
Why couldn't *I* be like that?
Why couldn't *I* be someone or something?
Why can't *I* do this right?
Why is it so; this life thing?
Why can't I be safe and sure and good and poor?
Why can't I be rounded, sounded, hopeful and great?
Why can't I search for the golden gate
in haste and turmoil with truth by my side?
Why can't I hold on to the one thing that matters?
Why is my life in rags and in tatters
battered and torn, raced and forlorn
without the sunshine on my lawn?
Why without something or someone
or both, troth this could be better
and yetter, it is, so called enough
to bluff the corners and buffer the story's
liking to a glory in the mind a nine stories
of love and failure, curtailed and mailer
beyond religion and recompense
sought only to listen and hear the wrong
seen only to do as the others do song

wasted and basted and blasted and sought
so sorrow has a bird called joy
in the fantastic of the full flow

*

Why can't I have the temperature to succumb to
the inner banks of laid-en fallow
a truth which proves the senses and sight; allowed?
Why can't I live in the day of night?
Why is it I can't put up with much?
why, it irritates and rankles
Why does it strangle and hate?
Why do the less and powerless depress?
Then why is only a word and why is wise
Why can't I be like the format or formula?
Why can't I at least fail for failing's sake?
Why do I question the formidable strengths
in sex and love and fancy and dancing
with vanity in the pride of all ego?
Why must I let go? day in and day out; regular routine like
when it is the fucking way
when it makes the fuckin' day
when it makes for a life lived
not when all does not exist
far far away ... in the unseen future
as the times tell of what is to be and how it all looks

Why don't I have the patience to pay?
Why do I ignore the hatred and stay
here in this, this that is, this time to be?
Why can't I honestly see
why the fucking joke's on me?
What will do as the masses join
same taste, same value, all principle
Why can't I change the destiny of mass victimisation
of chaos with a frightened control
of peace which hurts the soul
in hells of changes
which rearranges
the psyche to empower
a faithful race to flower –
covering its destructive with goodwill?
Why don't I know what I am saying?
When I reply to the conversation of strangers
where have the dead souls gone?
Why I cannot life-force the energy

*

Why I cannot life-force the energized
What have I done to deserve so much nothing?
When it is activist to leave most things be?
Ha! You may add – but fuck you …
Some things do not matter – a holy man's head on a platter
which leads me to another subject

of why; if seen from afar
the human would be seen as annoying?
A gloating superior covering all aspects
So glad to be, then sad to see
the way in which
it has to be done ... right and wrong
the way in which the destroyers
are happy, in glee, so smiley
when the enemy amongst all things
is present at the fullest extent
crawling over planet
climbing over aspects
if this is god-consciousness
then god is shit spirit.
Earth goddess
Then how irritating for the lost and beaten
to see the ignorant smile in their paradise
to see them wallow in the Babylonian cities
as the change is made – time is a fashion thing
time and fine and fun and frolic
depressing destroying soulless guile
when you die; they die – death is nearby ...
how irritating the almighty power
not to know – not to have to go – forget it!
To watch as the life and death way is worshipped
annoying this vermin – collected

a cancerous parasite – infested
an alien to the invested
the user blue
the who
the why
you.

*

I wrote the song *Tom Thumb* when I was 14. 1973. It has stayed with me all my life and I like to sing it when I'm drunk sometimes. I read about Malcolm White in the Yorkshire Evening press once and I thought how cruel it most be to hurt a small child like that. Tessa Maddocks; I'll never forget her. Bless her.

*

Many years later looking into the song, I realised Tom Thumb was in fact a dwarf. I have nothing against dwarfs and inaugurated the song into my novella *Death of Leader Rock* and his alter-ego cult punk band *Joker*.

May the light shine upon us all X

*

TOM THUMB *[Malcolm White]*

Malcolm White aged twenty
only four foot nine
didn't realise what he was doing
didn't realise what he had done …
I suppose he thought it was fun.

He strangled her, attempted sex
and slashed her neck with a knife
he strung her from a tree with a noose
didn't realise he was taking her life …

Nine years old, life to lead,
"Sir, can you tell me the time?"
no more life to lead for her
Tom Thumb you've committed a crime …

I'm sorry Tessa Maddocks.
I'm sorry, I really am.
You're gone, he's here,
But don't you fear…
He'll get what he deserves,
I hope they're not too soft …
I hope they hang the bastard,
hang him from a loft … !

Nine years old, life to lead
"Sir, can you tell me the time?"
No more life to lead for her
Tom Thumb you've committed a crime …

COME [SONG OF AVALON]

COME take me as I am *[Chorus]*
I'll understand.
Somewhere deep in my heart
Somewhere I can start ...
... and somewhere, where I feel
deep down inside of me
forever and a day;
eternally.

You and I, can watch the stars
as passers-by look to see
the love in our eyes
knowing we are
as passers-by; look above
and see a shining sky
in love ... Come!

COME take me as I am
I'll understand.
Somewhere deep in my heart
Somewhere I can start ...
... and somewhere, where I feel
deep down inside of me
forever and a day;
eternally.

Take me away from the madding fray
and say, what a day to remember
into night
light up the stage of love
inside out and above
come take me as I am

COME take me as I am
I'll understand.
Somewhere deep in my heart
Somewhere I can start ...
... and somewhere, where I feel
deep down inside of me
forever and a day;
eternally.

COME take me as I am
then the world can understand
there is a reason for being here
when you see yourself in the depth of soul
in the amazing corner of her eye
no tears, no cry, just joy
and somewhere; where I feel ... COME!

Take me as I am ... etc

*

Come [Song of Avalon] is an Arthurian ballad. Taken from the reaches of my heart on the Tor at Glastonbury; circa 2000.
It's operatic and 'zonk' like Operazonk; 'Zonk' being what was called about Bertolt Brecht and Kurt Weill songs of Germany. This is English opera and sings to the heart of betrayed love and a hope to regain some resemblance of trust and faith, when one is fucked.
Bless. Imagine. Gemini simple genius tune which crescendos with a great orchestra of voices; heavenly and eternal x

*

Also by Derek Peter Thornton

www.ingramcontent.com/pod-product-compliance
Lightning Source LLC
LaVergne TN
LVHW021400080426
835508LV00020B/2382